The Institute of Biology's
Studies in Biology no. 109

Lizards—A Study in Thermoregulation

R. A. Avery
B.Sc., Ph.D.
Lecturer in Zoology, University of Bristol

D1601063

University Park Press
Baltimore

© R. A. Avery, 1979

First published 1979 by Edward Arnold (Publishers) Limited
First Published in the U.S.A. in 1979 by University Park Press 233 East
Redwood Street Baltimore, Maryland 21202

Library of Congress Cataloging in Publication Data

Avery, Roger Anthony.
    Lizards, a study in thermoregulation.

(The Institute of Biology's studies in biology; no. 109)
    Includes index.
    1. Lizards—Physiology.   2. Body temperature—Regulation.
3. Reptiles—Physiology.   I. Title.   II. Series: Institute of Biology.
Studies in biology; no. 109.

QL666.L2A92   598.1/12/041   79-1237

ISBN 0-8391-0259-3

Printed in Great Britain

General Preface to the Series

Because it is no longer possible for one textbook to cover the whole field of biology while remaining sufficiently up to date, the Institute of Biology has sponsored this series so that teachers and students can learn about significant developments. The enthusiastic acceptance of 'Studies in Biology' shows that the books are providing authoritative views of biological topics.

The features of the series include the attention given to methods, the selected list of books for further reading and, wherever possible, suggestions for practical work.

Readers' comments will be welcomed by the Education Officer of the Institute.

1978   Institute of Biology
                                                   41 Queen's Gate
                                                   London SW7 5HU

Preface

Lizards are one of the most abundant groups of vertebrates and have successfully adapted to a wide range of environmental conditions. They are found in the hottest deserts, in the damp shade of tropical rain forests, on the pastures and moorlands of temperate lands, on mountains near the snow-line, and burrowing within the soil. They are particularly common in the warmer climates of the world, and have attracted increasing attention from ecologists and physiologists over the past twenty years.

One of the key aspects of lizard biology is the way in which these animals can maintain a relatively constant body temperature, not by metabolic means, but by adjusting their behaviour so that they make maximum use of external sources of heat. In contrast to other animals which function in this way, many species of lizards control their body temperature with a high degree of precision. This booklet examines how such control is achieved, and shows that other aspects of lizard ecology, behaviour and physiology are determined by thermoregulatory considerations. An understanding of these inter-relationships is of considerable intrinsic interest; it also helps to explain how warm-bloodedness might have evolved in mammals, birds, and perhaps dinosaurs.

Bristol, 1978   R.A.A.

Contents

1 Introduction

1.1 Evolution of lizards

Lizards are vertebrates and belong to the class Reptilia. Reptiles evolved from amphibians. Although animals in these two groups may look superficially rather similar (Linnaeus, the originator of modern scientific classification, did not distinguish between them), they have a number of important differences in structure and mode of organization. Reptiles have a scaly skin, which enables them to resist desiccation, and as a consequence, the skin is not used to any significant extent as a respiratory organ. They have a pair of lungs, which develop in the embryo and are retained throughout life (they do not, like amphibians, have an aquatic larval stage with gills). They produce large, yolky eggs which usually have a tough outer shell, and the embryo is surrounded by four membranes –the yolk sac, amnion, chorion and allantois. All of these characters are adaptations for life on land.

Reptiles first appeared during the Carboniferous period, at about the same time as insects and higher plants. The group showed enormous adaptive radiation during the Permian period and the succeeding Mesozoic era (the Age of Reptiles), but many kinds became extinct at the end of the Cretaceous. The order Squamata, which contains the lizards and snakes, appeared at about this time, and is the only group of reptiles which increased in numbers during the Tertiary. There are now approximately 3000 species of lizards and an equivalent number of snakes, whereas there are only 200 species of turtles and tortoises, and a mere 25 species of crocodiles.

1.2 The diversity of lizard species

There is no single character which distinguishes lizards from other groups of reptiles; definition is based on the structure of the bones of the skull, backbone and limbs. Understanding the classification of modern lizards also needs a detailed knowledge of comparative anatomy. The most primitive of the lizards which are alive today are believed to be the agamas (family Agamidae) of the Old World, and the iguanas (family Iguanidae) of the New. The lizards illustrated in Figs. 3-4, 5-3 and 7-2 are members of the Iguanidae. Most of the species are diurnal and in many parts of the tropics and subtropics they are very abundant –in some places, for example in parts of

Central America and some islands of the Caribbean, they are more numerous than birds or mammals. The Agamidae are ancestors of the chameleons (family Chamaeleontidae) of Africa, which are arboreal (they live in bushes and trees), have prehensile tails, long telescopic tongues which are used for catching flying insects, and remarkably well-developed abilities to change colour.

Almost equally primitive are the cosmopolitan geckos (family Gekkonidae, Fig. 6-2) which are small, often nocturnal, and have adhesive pads on the digits which make them extremely agile climbers. Many species enter houses, and some can run upside down across the ceiling.

Amongst the lizard groups which are generally considered to be more advanced are the skinks (family Scincidae). Many species are elongated, and some show a reduction or even complete loss of the limbs. This loss has occurred several times independently during the course of skink evolution and it may also be seen in the unrelated family Anguidae, which contains the 'glass snakes' and the 'slow-worm' as well as typical quadrupedal forms, and Amphisbaenidae, which is a family of burrowing lizards feeding mainly on earthworms. Other relatively advanced lizards include the families Lacertidae in the Old World (most of the common European lizards, including the viviparous lizard shown in Fig. 2-5, are lacertids), Teiidae in the New World, and Varanidae, which includes the large powerful monitor lizards or goannas of Africa, Asia and Australia. The Komodo Dragon, which is the largest species of lizard, is a monitor.

When the lizards of different parts of the world are compared, it is interesting to observe how species which are unrelated taxonomically may nevertheless be adapted to fill similar ecological niches, in rather the same kind of way that marsupial mammals in Australia have radiated in parallel with eutherian mammals elsewhere. One of the most striking examples of such convergence is the morphological and ecological similarity of the horned 'toads' (family Iguanidae; see Fig. 5-3) of the deserts of western North America with the 'spiny devil' (family Agamidae) of Australia. There are more species of lizards in the deserts of Australia than in desert habitats elsewhere, perhaps because of the lack of competition with higher mammals.

2 Thermoregulation—the Key to Lizard Biology

2.1 Thermoregulation and behaviour

It has become customary to divide animals, from a physiological standpoint, into two major groups: those which are cold-blooded or *poikilothermic* and those which are warm-blooded or *homeothermic*. This is a useful classification, but like most attempts to impose a simple intellectual order on nature, it has disadvantages. One of these is that so-called cold-blooded animals may at times have body temperatures as high as, or even higher, than those of warm-blooded birds and mammals. For this reason a slightly different distinction is sometimes made: that between *endotherms*, which generate their body heat internally from metabolic energy, and *ectotherms*, which obtain any heat which their bodies may contain over and above that of the general environment, primarily from external sources such as direct solar radiation, or from hot rocks or bark, or (rarely) from hot springs and geysers.

Lizards fall within the second category; they are ectotherms. Often, however, they maintain a surprisingly high body temperature. They do so by moving into the sunshine or onto hot rocks when they are too cool, and into the shade when they are too hot. This kind of regulation is often called *behavioural thermoregulation*. The body temperature may be maintained by this means at a relatively constant level—provided that the sun remains shining.

Lizards are not the only animals which thermoregulate in this way. Various species of butterflies, moths, bees, dragonflies, locusts, spiders, fishes and amphibians, as well as other reptiles such as snakes, crocodiles, tortoises and turtles, may show thermoregulatory behaviour; but in nearly all of these cases, the control which is achieved is less precise.

The basic features of behavioural thermoregulation in lizards were first described in a classic series of papers by R. B. Cowles and C. M. Bogert (see COWLES and *bogert, 1944,* and BOGERT, 1949), but like many important discoveries in biology, this one was preceded by a number of relevant observations by people who did not entirely appreciate the significance of what they saw. WEESE (1919) noticed that horned toads (*Phrynosoma* spp.—they are lizards and not amphibians, despite their vernacular name) in New Mexico were most active when the air or substrate temperatures were at about 36°C. Weese did not actually measure the temperature of the lizards he studied, but twenty years later, several Russian and German workers recorded the temperatures of lizards and showed that during the day they were nearly always above that of the surrounding air, even at very high altitudes near the snow line in the Caucasus Mountains (see Chapter 6).

Many people have subsequently worked on thermoregulation in reptiles. It is interesting to see how the increasing sophistication of techniques which are available has improved the accuracy with which measurements can be made. The first important development was the introduction of a mercury thermometer with a bulb which was small enough to insert into the cloaca of a small lizard, and which had a sufficiently low thermal capacity that it responded rapidly, so that the temperature of an animal which had been captured in the field could be recorded almost instantaneously. This was superseded by the thermistor, which is even smaller. It is now possible to implant a temperature-sensitive radiotelemetry device (the smallest of which weighs about 0.5 g) into the body cavity of medium-sized and large lizards and so continuously record the body temperature without restraining the animal. An example of the kind of record which can be made in this way is shown in Fig. 2-1. But the implanted device is still a bulky foreign body in a small lizard and efforts are now being made to record subcutaneous temperatures by monitoring microwave emission at about 3 GHz with radiometers of the kind which have been developed for studying radioastronomy.

Increased understanding of thermoregulation has led to a jargon which has become confused, and it is often necessary to define terms

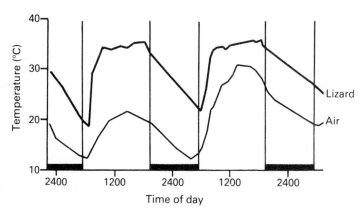

Fig. 2-1 Body temperature of a free-living lace monitor (*Varanus varius*) recorded continuously over a 2½-day period with a radiotelemetry device. The temperature of the air is also shown. (Adapted from STEBBINS, R. C. and BARWICK, R. E., *Copeia,* **1968**, 541–7.)

rather carefully in order to make quite clear the sense in which they are being used (this problem is not, unfortunately, confined to the study of thermoregulation – it bedevils most areas of science).

One of the earliest concepts was that of the *preferred body temperature* (PBT). This is the temperature which a lizard will select if it is placed in a cage containing a range of different regions from hot to cold. Some authors dislike the use of the word 'preferred' and substitute *eccritic*, which is derived from the Greek word *ekkriton*, to select. The idea of a PBT is related to the physiological concept of homeostasis; it is often assumed that the PBT is the optimum for the animal's physiological processes, and notably for its enzymes. This may sometimes be the case, for example the optimum temperature for the activity of myosin ATP-ase is similar to the maximum activity temperatures in several species of American lizards. Heart rate and contractility of heart muscle correlate with activity temperature; but the activity of alkaline phosphatase does not. The PBT of each species tends to be constant, although it may vary over the geographical range. The PBTs of different species, however, show considerable variation (Table 1).

In some species of lizards the PBT also changes with different seasons and it is sometimes possible to predict the PBT at any given time. TURNER, MEDICA and KOWALEWSKY (1976) made a careful study of the side-blotched lizard, *Uta stansburiana*, in Nevada, and showed that the PBT (they called it T_{max}) varied approximately as a sine function between limits of 32°C in mid-summer and 38°C in mid-winter. The PBT on any given day is given empirically by the relation

$$T_{max} = 35 + 3\sin(K + 314)$$

where $K = 0$ on 1 March and the days of the year are numbered consecutively thereafter.

A careful examination of the body temperatures of lizards in the field often reveals that they may function for much of the time at temperatures which are below, or less often above, the PBT. Figure 2-1 shows that during the day, the body temperature of an Australian monitor lizard *Varanus varius* was maintained for most of the time between 34 and 37°C. At night and in the early morning it fell to 20°C. A similar diurnal pattern of temperature regulation has been recorded in many species of lizards. The body temperatures of viviparous lizards, *Lacerta vivipara*, which were kept in an outdoor enclosure in England, on a hot sunny day in June, are shown in Fig. 2-2. During the day, temperature was maintained at 27–33°C, but at night it fell to 15–17°C. Note that in *L. vivipara* the night temperature was the same as that of the ambient air, whereas in *V. varius* it was well above this level. The reasons for this difference are explained in Chapter 3.

Table 1 Preferred body temperatures (PBTs) of eleven species of lizards.

Species	Location	(0°C)	Methods
Anguis fragilis (slow-worm)	England	23	Temperature gradient in laboratory. Thermistor in cloaca
Nephurus laevissimus (gecko)	Australia	18 (winter) 26 (summer)	Field. Mercury thermometer in cloaca
Panaspis kitsoni (skink)	Ivory Coast	27	Field. Mercury thermometer in cloaca
Lacerta vivipara (viviparous lizard)	England	30	Open air vivarium. Mercury thermometer in cloaca
Tropidurus albermarlensis (lava lizard)	Galapagos Is.	34.5	Field. Mercury thermometer in cloaca
Amblyrhynchus cristatus (marine iguana)	Galapagos Is.	35*	Field. Thermistor in cloaca
Podarcis sicula (ruin lizard)	Italy	35	Field. Thermistor in cloaca
Amphibolurus barbatus (bearded dragon)	Australia	35	Field. Mercury thermometer in oesophagus
Varanus varius (lace monitor or goanna)	Australia	35.5	Field. Radiotelemetry
Amphibolurus inermis (desert dragon)	Simpson Desert, Australia	41.5	Field. Mercury thermometer and thermistor in cloaca
Dipsosaurus dorsalis (desert iguana)	Mojave Desert, U.S.A.	38–43	Field. Mercury thermometer in cloaca

* temperature when on land. The body temperatures of swimming iguanas are much lower.

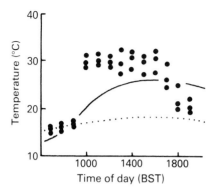

Fig. 2-2 Body temperatures of three viviparous lizards (*Lacerta vivipara*) maintained in an outdoor enclosure. The figure also shows air temperatures at ground level (continuous line) and in the burrow into which the animals could retreat (dotted line). (AVERY, R. A. (1971). *J. Anim. Ecol.*, **40**, 351–65.)

The range of body temperatures at which a lizard species may show active behaviour such as hunting, feeding and fighting is often called the *activity temperature* or (inaccurately) the *mean body temperature*. HUEY and SLATKIN (1976) think that since the optimum activity temperature may not be the same as the optimum physiological temperature, the body temperature which a lizard will maintain in any situation represents a compromise between the two. They define the optimum activity temperature as that at which the animal maximizes its energy intake, i.e. obtains the greatest amount of food with the greatest efficiency. This is an interesting idea, but it is difficult to test experimentally.

A lizard may gain heat from the environment in a number of different ways. The most important are direct absorption of solar radiation, or conduction from hot air or a hot substrate. It may lose heat by radiation from the body surface, by convection, by conduction to a cool substrate, and by evaporative cooling. Heat exchanges by all of these means may be seen in different lizard species. Those which gain their heat primarily by direct absorption of solar radiation are called *basking heliotherms* (Greek: *helios*, sun). Basking is obviously of great importance to those lizard species in temperate climates which maintain a high PBT (and the majority do –see Chapter 6) and they may spend a considerable part of the day simply lying in the sun. Endeavouring to study this behaviour in the field is often more difficult than it might seem, because the animals may have a number of different basking sites. They frequently disappear whilst they are moving between sites; or one of the sites may be obscured by

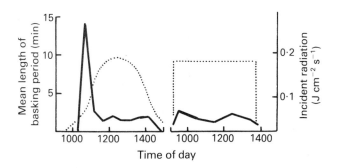

Fig. 2-3 Basking behaviour of *Lacerta vivipara* when exposed to two different regimes of irradiation (dotted lines) from an incubator lamp. (Project data of J. A. Boreham. With permission from AVERY, 1976. Copyright by Academic Press Inc. (London) Ltd.)

rocks or overhanging vegetation. J. A. Boreham, in carrying out an undergraduate project at Bristol University, circumvented this problem by keeping *Lacerta vivipara* in a large cage and suspending a 250 W incubator lamp over them to simulate the sun. She carefully calibrated the radiation from the bulb, and varied the voltage applied to it in such a way that the radiation followed a sine wave which was approximately equivalent to natural solar radiation. She then observed the basking behaviour of the lizards at different times in the cycle. A typical result is shown in Fig. 2-3. Note that in the early part of the cycle, the lizards spent up to 15 minutes at a time in basking.

The mean activity temperature of *L. vivipara* is 30–31°C (Fig. 2-2), and if the body temperature falls below about 25°C, the animals are not able to feed efficiently. Clearly it will take a lizard a shorter time to warm up to its activity temperature during the middle of the day than in the early morning or late afternoon. This will determine the time at which it first emerges from its night retreat. *L. vivipara* can first be seen in mid-summer in Britain at about 0745 GMT. AVERY and MCARDLE (1973) have shown that this is the time at which a graph of heating rate against time begins to flatten out (Fig. 2-4a). If a lizard emerges before this time, it will have to spend a long time basking, and this will be a disadvantage because it will increase the time during which it is immobile and exposed to predators. These include man. Hence it is easier to catch *L. vivipara* in the morning whilst they are basking than at other times. But this is not true for all species; RAND (1964) has demonstrated that *Anolis lineatopus*, which is an arboreal lizard found in Jamaica, becomes shyer to compensate for the increased vulnerability, and is *more* difficult to catch whilst it is basking. If a *L. vivipara* emerges after the optimum time, it will have wasted a

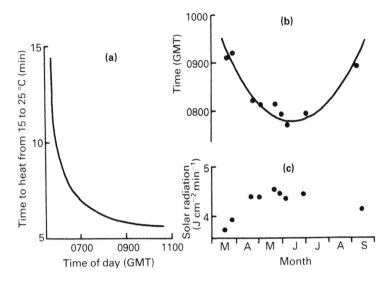

Fig. 2-4 *Lacerta vivipara*: heating rates (**a**), times of morning emergence (**b**) and calculated solar radiation at the time of emergence (**c**). (From AVERY and MCARDLE, 1973.)

period during which it could have been maintaining the PBT and so hunting for food. During the spring and autumn, the morning sun is less intense and so *L. vivipara* emerge later (Fig. 2-4b, c). The results shown in Fig. 2-4b relate to days when the sun is not obscured by cloud. Poor weather has a profound effect on the behaviour of lizards, but this has not been studied systematically and would make an excellent project. Not all species behave in the same kind of way as *L. vivipara*. For example, horned toads in the deserts of the south-west U.S.A. emerge from the sand before sunrise, at a constant time which is independent of temperature; this is an example of an endogenous rhythm (HEATH, 1962). Another interesting project would be to study the factors which determine the times at which lizards retreat into their hiding places after the activity period. These times are much more variable than times of emergence, and in *L. vivipara* they seem to be less dependent on temperature. The amount of food which has been eaten during the day might be important, but preliminary experiments have given results which are inconclusive on this point.

   Lizards which are basking adopt quite distinct postures. They sprawl on the ground, with legs outstretched, and flatten the ribcage, so increasing the surface area which can be exposed to the sun. *L. vivipara* will often turn their palms outwards (see Fig. 2-5) and make

Fig. 2-5 *Lacerta vivipara*. The lizard in the upper photograph is basking. In order to maximize the surface area which is exposed to the rays of the sun, the body is flattened and the limbs are sprawled sideways. The forelimbs are raised off the ground. The lower photograph shows the same animal in an alert posture whilst hunting; the body has a rounded cross-section, and the head is raised. (Photographs by courtesy of M. A. Linley.)

scrabbling movements with their limbs, but the significance of this behaviour is not understood. When they have achieved the activity temperature, they stop basking. Some species of lizards will then begin actively foraging for food, others will seek a look-out where they remain immobile, waiting for suitable food to come into their field of view. In either case, the rate at which they absorb heat is likely to be reduced and they may lose heat. A time will come when their temperature has fallen to the lower limit of the activity range, and then they must bask again. The daily behaviour pattern is an alternation of periods of activity with periods of basking. Such species have been called *shuttling heliotherms*, because they shuttle into and out of the sun. The frequency and duration of basking will depend on the intensity of the solar radiation (see Fig. 2-3) and also on the range of the activity temperature of the species. Some species maintain a fairly constant body temperature, others will allow it to fluctuate within quite wide limits. *Anolis cristatellus* in the forests of Puerto Rico adapts its behaviour in this respect according to the nature of its immediate surroundings. If an individual lives at the edge of the forest, or in a clearing, it behaves as a shuttling heliotherm; but if it is within the deep forest, there will be very little direct sunlight available to it and it ceases thermoregulating and so the body temperature fluctuates with that of the surrounding air (Fig. 2-6).

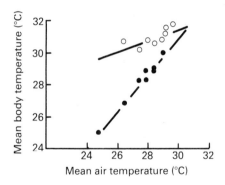

Fig. 2-6   Body temperatures of *Anolis cristatellus* from deep forest (●) and open habitats (○) in Puerto Rico. (Modified from HUEY and SLATKIN, 1976.)

Shuttling is probably the most important kind of thermoregulatory behaviour in lizards which inhabit temperate climates, and in those species which are found in open, sparsely-vegetated habitats such as savannah, desert and forest clearings. But in other species, control of heating and cooling is primarily by means of body posture and orientation (Fig. 2-7); these are often called *posturing heliotherms*.

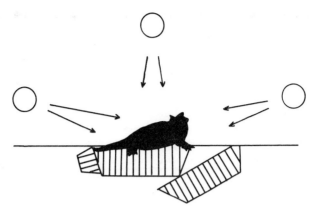

Fig. 2-7 Diagrammatic representation of orientation behaviour by a horned toad (*Phrynosoma* sp.). Large differences in the amount of solar radiation impinging on the body result when the animal shifts its position. Facing the sun on the right results in exposure of the body to a radiant heat load which is proportional to the shadow on the left. Facing away from the sun on the left results in the shadow on the right. The shadow immediately below the animal results from positive normal orientation. (From an original drawing by R. B. Cowles, modified with permission from HEATH, 1965.)

The distinction is not a hard-and-fast one; many species use both methods. Shuttling and postural changes may also be used to control the rate at which heat is lost. This is of greatest importance to lizards in very hot climates and is discussed in Chapter 5.

Yet other species obtain a substantial part of their heat by conduction from hot rocks and bark; this is only effective in maintaining a high temperature at latitudes in which there is intense solar radiation. Such species are called *thigmotherms* (Greek: *thigma*, touch). A particularly interesting kind of thigmothermy is to be seen in an Australian gecko, *Gehyra variegata*. This species is nocturnal, and the lizards usually forage for food during the three hours following sunset. During the day they remain hidden, frequently beneath the bark of tree stumps. Soon after dawn they move around the trunk, beneath the bark where it is peeling away from the wood, so that they are on the north side and they then lie there with their bellies pressed against the underside of the bark. Since it faces the sun, this is the warmest part of the stump. The lizards remain on the north side until about mid-day, but then the heat becomes too intense and they return to the cooler side. The significance of this behaviour is not known, but it may be that the high temperatures which the animals seek during the day increase digestive efficiency (BUSTARD, 1967).

Not all species of lizards regulate their body temperatures in the precise ways which have been described. Individuals of the Californian silvery legless lizard, *Anniella pulchra*, spend their entire life burrowing in the soil. They tend to burrow deeper in the summer months, but it is not known whether this is for thermoregulatory reasons, or because of migrations of the invertebrates which form their food supply. Body temperatures in these lizards are very variable, but the mean is usually near 20°C. The European slow-worm, *Anguis fragilis*, which is another legless lizard, also has a variable body temperature; in a thermal gradient in the laboratory it has a PBT of approximately 20°C, like *Anniella*. It is active primarily at dawn and dusk, but may sometimes be seen basking during the day. Its behaviour is something of an enigma, and much more needs to be learnt about it.

2.2 The control of thermoregulatory behaviour

How does a lizard monitor its body temperature? And how does it integrate that knowledge into appropriate patterns of behaviour? We do not know the detailed answers to these questions. It is certain that a region of the brain called the hypothalamus is involved; some of the ways in which this may function in mammals are described by HARDY (1976). Implantation of microelectrodes into the brain of the Australian blue-tongued skink *Tiliqua scincoides* has shown that there are both heat-sensitive and cold-sensitive neurons, i.e. neurons which increase their firing-rate in response to increasing or decreasing temperatures. Many other neurons are not temperature-sensitive. There must also be thermal receptors in the skin, since otherwise postural heliothermy and thigmothermy would not be possible except on a very inefficient 'trial and error' basis.

Recently, BERK and HEATH (1975) have studied thermoregulatory behaviour of the American desert iguana, *Dipsosaurus dorsalis*, in a piece of apparatus called a shuttlebox, and have combined their results with what is known about the nervous system to devise a hypothetical model showing how the PBT might be maintained. A shuttlebox is simply a cage in which one end is kept slightly hotter than the animal's PBT and the other end slightly cooler. In order to thermoregulate, the lizard must shuttle from one end of the box to the other. If a thermistor is inserted into the cloaca of the lizard and the wires suspended from the roof of the cage with a spring to maintain light tension so that the animal does not become entangled, it is possible to record the body temperature continuously. There are two set points which determine the shuttling behaviour; these are the temperatures at which the animal seeks to warm itself and to cool itself (Fig. 2-8).

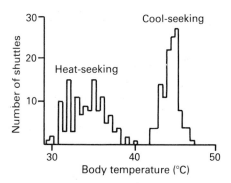

Fig. 2-8 Body temperatures at which a desert iguana (*Dipsosaurus dorsalis*) seeks the hot or cool end of a shuttlebox. (BERK and HEATH, 1975.)

A simplified diagram of Berk and Heath's model is shown in Fig. 2-9. The essential features of the homeostatic brain mechanism is that there are both excitatory and inhibitory synapses. The excitatory synapses are activated from the hot and cold receptors in the hypothalamus, and the inhibitory synapses from the temperature receptors in the skin, which act via a part of the brain called the reticular formation. The level of excitation of the inhibitory synapses is also determined by other environmental factors, such as the time of day, and also by internal factors such as thirst, hunger and the amount of previous activity.

If the animal is on the hot side of the shuttlebox, it will warm up and this will result in an increase in the firing rate of the heat-sensitive receptors in the hypothalamus, whose axons lead to motor neurons which initiate cold-seeking behaviour. At the same time, increase in the firing rate of the skin receptors results in *inhibition* of the temperature-insensitive neuron, so the inhibition which this exerts on the motor neuron will be reduced. Ultimately a threshold will be reached and the motor neuron will fire. The lizard will now seek the cold side of the shuttlebox and will begin to cool. Nerve impulses from the heat receptors will decrease and from the cold receptors will increase. When the threshold of stimulation for the motor neuron which initiates heat-seeking behaviour is reached, this will fire and the animal will shuttle again, this time to the hot side of the box.

At the end of the day, the lizard stops seeking a high temperature and becomes inactive. This could be effected by an increase in the firing rate of the temperature-insensitive neuron, mediated via the reticular formation, which would inhibit the motor neuron for heat-seeking behaviour so that its threshold was above that of the maximum firing rate of the hypothalmic cold receptor. The model shown

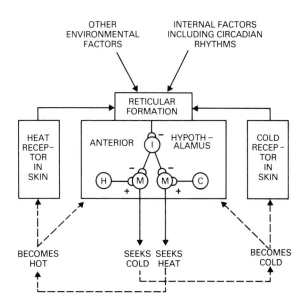

Fig. 2-9 Simplified diagram of the neural network for a thermoregulatory control mechanism in *Dipsosaurus dorsalis*. Neural connections are shown as continuous lines. Synapses are represented as stimulatory (+) or inhibitory (−). Neurons in the anterior hypothalamus are represented as temperature-insensitive (I), heat-sensitive (H), cold-sensitive (C) or motor neurons (M). (Modified from BERK and HEATH, 1975.)

in Fig. 2-9 is almost certainly an oversimplification, and it might be incorrect; but if attempts to refine it lead to an increased understanding of the complexities involved, then like all such interim hypotheses, it will have served a useful purpose.

One of the complexities which a complete theory of thermoregulation will have to account for is the involvement of the pineal eye. This structure, sometimes called the parietal or third eye, is found in many lizard species, but it is absent in some of those which live near the Equator and also from most species of geckos. It lies beneath the skin at the top of the head and has a functional retina and a nerve to the brain, but it does not have muscles or an eyelid and it cannot accommodate. Its precise function is uncertain, but it is believed to be a kind of radiation dosimeter which helps to synchronize daily and seasonal cycles of activity with changes in daylength or intensity of solar radiation. Most of its actions are inhibitory. A lizard from which it has been removed surgically, or in which it has been covered with an opaque shield, may show some of the following responses (they vary from species to species): increased activity of the thyroid

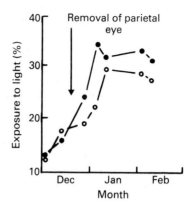

Fig. 2-10 Effects of parietalectomy on the frequency of exposure of *Xantusia vigilis* to light. (●) experimental, (○) control. (From STEBBINS, R. C. (1970). *Copeia*, **1970**, 261–70.)

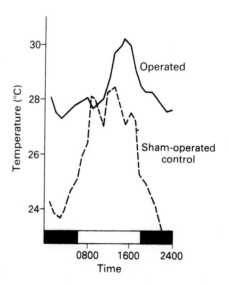

Fig. 2-11 Temperatures selected by parietalectomized and control anoles (*Anolis carolinensis*) in a thermal gradient. (HUTCHISON, V. A. and KOSH, R. J. (1974). *Oecologia* (*Berl.*), **16**, 173–7.)

gland; a speeded-up reproductive cycle; increased locomotor activity; increased exposure to sunlight. Figure 2-10 shows changes in the behaviour of a Californian lizard, *Xantusia vigilis*, after removal of the eye (parietalectomy). The animals were placed in a box which had an even temperature throughout, but one end was brightly lit and the other shaded. The parietalectomized animals spent more time than the controls at the light end of the box. A similar kind of result was seen when the parietal eye of *Lacerta vivipara* from Britain was covered with a small piece of aluminium foil; each of the experimental lizards spent more time basking than the controls (unpublished student project work of M. E. Appleby). In the American 'chameleon', *Anolis carolinensis*, which is a non-basking lizard, removal of the third eye caused the animal to seek higher temperatures in a thermal gradient (Fig. 2-11).

3 Physiology and the Evolution of Homeothermy

Animals which thermoregulate by behavioural means must often function at a wider range of body temperature than either non-thermoregulators or homeotherms. The adaptations which enable them to do so are of considerable interest. Some enzymes in lizards appear to function *in vitro* most efficiently at the PBT of the species from which they have been extracted, but others do not (Chapter 2); not enough is known about either lizards or enzymes to interpret the reasons for this difference.

The metabolic rates of lizards are similar to those of other poikilotherms at the same temperatures. More than 100 studies on lizard metabolism have been published, the first as long ago as 1849. They include determinations of oxygen consumption, carbon dioxide production, or heat production (the latter is rather difficult to measure and has not often been attempted). The conditions under which these experiments have been carried out has varied; the animals may have been active or resting, or have been well-fed or starved. If one wishes to make comparisons, it is necessary to select studies in which these factors have been controlled and *standard metabolic rate* is usually used for this purpose. The standard metabolic rate is usually considered to be that which is seen in a resting animal during the inactive phase of its diurnal cycle and the animal should be in a 'post-absorptive state', i.e. it should not be digesting food and so should not have been fed immediately prior to the experiment. There has been much controversy about the exact definition of these conditions.

The standard metabolic rates of lizards increase with increasing temperature; like so many biological processes, they follow van't Hoff's Law, which states that the rate of a biochemical reaction usually doubles for every increase in temperature of approximately 10°C. BENNETT and DAWSON (1976) have calculated the following equations which specify standard metabolic rates at three different temperatures:

$$20°C: \quad M = 0.096W^{0.80} \tag{1}$$
$$30°C: \quad M = 0.240W^{0.83} \tag{2}$$
$$37°C: \quad M = 0.424W^{0.82} \tag{3}$$

M is the metabolic rate expressed as ml of oxygen consumed per hour and W is the live weight of the lizard in g. Equations (1) to (3) are in the form of power-series, because metabolism relates exponentially, not directly, to body weight. This is characteristic of the resting metabolism of nearly all organisms from bacteria to man, although the exponent is commonly nearer to 0.75 than 0.8.

If both sides of a power-series equation are converted to logarithms and values for the two variables are plotted on graph paper, they form a straight line. Thus equation (3) becomes

$$\log M = \log 0.424 + 0.82 \log W \qquad (4)$$

It is often more useful, however, to express metabolism as a rate *per unit weight*; in order to do this we divide by W, i.e.

$$\log(M/W) = \log 0.424 + (0.82 - 1) \log W \qquad (5)$$

Equation (5) is plotted in Fig. 3-1 and for comparison the figure also shows the weight-specific metabolism of birds and mammals; it can be seen that the latter are five to ten times higher. The precise difference depends on the body weight at which the comparison is made. The heat production of a guinea pig, for example, is six times greater than that of an Australian bearded dragon, *Amphibolurus barbatus*, of the same size and with the same body temperature (37°C). The difference between humming-birds or shrews and small lizards of equivalent size is even greater.

The reason why a lizard, when it is maintaining a high body temperature, has a lower metabolic rate than a mammal or a bird is that heat needed to maintain the temperature difference between the body and the environment comes, in the lizard, primarily from thermal radiation, whereas in the mammal or bird it is internally generated. It is interesting that recent measurements of the specific

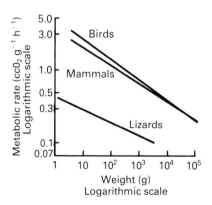

Fig. 3-1 Resting metabolism of lizards at 37°C compared with the metabolism of birds and mammals. (With permission from BENNETT and DAWSON (1976). Copyright by Academic Press Inc. (London) Ltd.)

activities of aerobic enzymes from the liver and skeletal muscles of lizards and rats have shown that they are higher in the rat. This is not because rat enzymes are more efficient, but because the concentration of mitochondria is greater –there are more of them.

The metabolism of a lizard does, of course, generate some heat, but because the animals do not have fur, feathers or the extensive deposits of subcutaneous fat which insulate homeotherms, it is dissipated very rapidly. Only in the largest of lizards, which have lower surface: volume ratios and so lose heat relatively slowly, does it increase the body temperature to a measurable extent. Even in these, however, the temperature can only be maintained about $1-2°C$ above that of the ambient air and only whilst the animal is active. A well-known exception to this general rule is that the Indian Python, *Python molurus*, can raise its body temperature when it is incubating its eggs by as much as $7°C$, provided that it maintains a continuous series of muscular contractions. The cost of this heating is high –the oxygen consumption of the incubating python is nine times greater than the basal metabolic rate.

Although metabolic heat is a negligible factor in the maintenance of body temperature in most reptiles, it does have some effect on thermoregulatory processes. This can be demonstrated by cooling a lizard in a refrigerator, then removing it and measuring its heating rate in hot air; and then by reversing the conditions and measuring the cooling rate of a hot lizard in cool air. If a dead lizard is used in the experiment, the heating and cooling rates for any temperature difference are the same. But if the animal is alive, it heats faster than it cools. Experiments of this kind have been carried out with a number of lizard species. One of the most thorough was an investigation of thermal regulation in *Amphibolurus barbatus* performed at the University of Queensland by BARTHOLOMEW and TUCKER (1963). The heating and cooling rates of the animals in chambers maintained at $40°C$ and $20°C$ respectively are shown in Fig. 3-2.

A living bearded dragon heated about 1.3 times faster than it cooled. This difference could have a number of causes; amongst the more important are:

(a) differences in thermal conductance due to change in the flow of blood in the skin;
(b) the contribution of metabolic heat;
(c) differences in body shape or posture;
(d) differences in evaporative cooling;
(e) differences in emissivity due to any change in the colour of the skin.

Bartholomew and Tucker showed that the last three of these factors were negligible in the conditions of the experiment (their importance

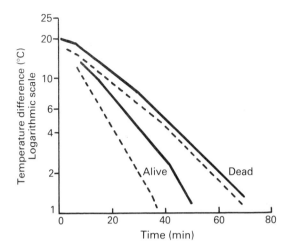

Fig. 3-2 The rates at which a bearded dragon (*Amphibolurus barbatus*) cools from 40°C (—) and heats from 20°C (---). The ordinate shows the difference between body and ambient temperatures. (From BARTHOLOMEW and TUCKER (1963). With the permission of the University of Chicago Press.)

in lizards which live in hot deserts is discussed in Chapter 5). The question then arose 'how much of the difference between heating and cooling rates is accounted for by metabolic heat'? This can be answered in the following way:

the cooling rate of a dead lizard (dH/dt) is given by Newton's Law of Cooling, which can be written as

$$\frac{dH}{dt} = C(T_B - T_A) \tag{6}$$

where

C = thermal conductance,
T_B = body temperature of lizard,
T_A = temperature of the ambient air.

If the specific heat of lizard tissue is denoted by K, then equation (6) can be written

$$\frac{dT_B}{dt} = \frac{C}{K}(T_B - T_A) \tag{7}$$

and this integrates to

$$\log(T_B - T_A) = \log E + \frac{Ct}{K}\log e \tag{8}$$

where E is a constant of integration and t is time. If $\log(T_B - T_A)$ is plotted on a graph against time, the slope of the curve will equal $(C \log e)/K$. Bartholomew and Tucker measured the specific heat of lizard tissue and showed that it was equal to 0.82. The conductance can then be calculated from

$$C = (\text{slope} \times 0.82)/\log e \qquad (9)$$

In a living lizard, the apparent conductance will be greater than that in a dead one, because of the contribution of metabolic heat (M). If we call this apparent conductance C', then by analogy with equation (7),

$$\frac{dT_B}{dt} = \frac{C'}{K}(T_B - T_A) \qquad (10)$$

The rates of heat production and heat loss may be equated algebraically, i.e.

$$\frac{dH}{dt} = M + \text{heat loss} \qquad (11)$$

Now by definition,

$$\text{heat loss} = C(T_B - T_A) \qquad (12)$$

Combining equations (11) and (12),

$$\frac{dH}{dt} = M + C(T_B - T_A) \qquad (13)$$

or

$$\frac{dT_B}{dt} = \frac{M + C(T_B - T_A)}{K} \qquad (14)$$

Equating equations (10) and (14)

$$\frac{M + C(T_B - T_A)}{K} = \frac{C'}{K}(T_B - T_A)$$

$$\therefore \ C = C' - \frac{M}{T_B - T_A} \qquad (15)$$

At any given temperature, the apparent conductance C' can be determined fron equation (9) and M determined by measurement of the oxygen consumption; the values are then substituted in equation (15) to calculate the actual thermal conductance C. Similar measurements and calculations can be carried out for heating lizards. The results of these experiments are shown in Table 2. It can be seen that

Table 2 Thermal conductance $(\mathrm{J\,g^{-1}h^{-1}{}^\circ C^{-1}})$ of *Amphibolurus barbatus*. Figures are the mean values of three determinations carried out at different temperatures. (Adapted from BARTHOLOMEW and TUCKER (1963). With permission from the University of Chicago Press.)

Apparent thermal conductance (C')		Actual (corrected) thermal conductance (C)	
Heating lizard	Cooling lizard	Heating lizard	Cooling lizard
15.46	11.89	14.74	12.10

apparent thermal conductance, C', was greater when a lizard was heating than when it was cooling. Correcting the conductances for metabolism reduced the difference between the values of C' and C by only 25%; i.e. metabolic heat accounted for only one quarter of the difference in heating and cooling rates and other physiological factors for 75%. Changes in the blood circulation are probably the most important of these 'other physiological factors'. Examples of such adaptations are changes in (*a*) heart rate, (*b*) peripheral blood flow and (*c*) various kinds of 'shunts'.

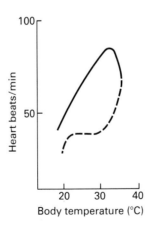

Fig. 3-3 Relation between heat rate and body temperature in a marine iguana (*Amblyrhynchus cristatus*) during heating (—) and cooling (---) in water. (From BARTHOLOMEW, G. A. and LASIEWSKI, R. C. (1965). *Comp. Biochem. Physiol.*, **16**, 573–82.)

Experiments with the Galapagos marine iguana, *Amblyrhynchus cristatus*, have shown how heart-rate may effect thermoregulation. If an animal is heated, the rate increases; if it is cooled, it decreases, but at a more rapid rate (Fig. 3-3). This has the effect of decreasing blood flow and so conserving heat, when the animal is cooling. When the animal is heating up, however, the increased blood flow increases the rate of conduction from the skin to the tissues and so increases the rate of heating. Changes in peripheral blood flow, which are caused by vasoconstriction or vasodilation of capillaries under sympathetic control, augment these processes; they have been recorded in a number of larger species, including the Central American iguana, *Iguana iguana*, and the Australian monitor, *Varanus varius*. *Iguana* is illustrated in Fig. 3-4. If these lizards are transferred from a container at 45°C, which is the maximum temperature that they will tolerate, to one at 10°C, then the superficial muscles in the legs and the tail cool to the lower temperature within about 15 minutes; but the deep body tissues do not finally reach 10°C until more than six hours later.

The subject of blood 'shunts' is particularly complex. Reptiles, unlike birds and mammals, have a connection between the left and right ventricles of the heart and they have both right and left systemic

Fig. 3-4 Common iguana (*Iguana iguana*). (Photograph by courtesy of M. A. Linley.)

arches. It is thus potentially possible to alter relative rates of blood flow to the lungs, head or body and it is believed that some lizards can alter these in appropriate ways to help maximize heat gain or minimize heat loss. There is also evidence that the blood vessels in the head may act as rather elaborate heat exchangers, with counterflow between the internal carotid artery and the internal jugular vein controlled by sphincter muscles around the latter. The animal hence has some control over the relative temperatures of the head and body (HEATH, 1966). Such modifications in the blood vessels are not confined to reptiles: fast-swimming fishes such as the bluefin tunny (*Thunnus thynnus*), in which the heat-exchangers are sheets of intermeshed blood vessels called 'retia', retain some of the metabolic heat which is generated by their powerful body muscles in a rather similar way (CAREY and TEAL, 1969).

Endothermic birds and mammals differ from ectotherms such as lizards in having higher standard metabolic rates. A further fundamental difference between them is that if the ambient temperature is reduced, endotherms increase their metabolic rate to compensate for the increased heat loss. The increment due to a cold environment has been called 'regulatory non-shivering thermogenesis'. An additional contribution to the heat budget may be made by shivering. Ectothermic lizards under similar conditions simply allow body temperature, and hence metabolic rate, to fall.

When the animals are active, yet another difference becomes apparent. This is in the relative contributions of aerobic and anaerobic metabolic pathways to their energy requirements. Aerobic respiration enables mammals and birds to maintain quite high levels of muscular activity for long periods. Anaerobic glycolysis is reserved for short, intense bursts of activity, each of which is followed by a period of 'oxygen debt'. In lizards, most of the energy for vigorous activity comes from glycolysis. This is because their relatively inefficient respiratory and circulatory systems limit the rate at which oxygen can be supplied to the tissues and also because the enzymes of the tricarboxylic acid cycle are more sensitive to changes in temperature than those of the Embden-Myerhof pathway. Glycolysis is quite efficient for short periods at high temperatures; it yields between 0.6 and $1.3 \, \text{J g}^{-1}$ in both mammals and lizards, and maximum running speeds in small mammals and small lizards are approximately the same.

The extent to which a lizard is utilizing glycolytic pathways at any time can be determined by measuring the concentration of the end-product, lactic acid, in the blood. In a resting reptile, this is usually present at a concentration of $0.04-0.2 \, \text{mg ml}^{-1}$. Moderate activity increases the concentration by a factor of between two and five times; an iguana walking on a treadmill had blood lactate concentrations of

$0.28-0.48$ mg ml^{-1}. Maximum activity increases the concentration still more; when an iguana was stimulated to run as fast as it was able, by applying gentle electric shocks, the concentration rose to more than 1.0 mg ml^{-1}. This quantity of acid causes a marked reduction in the pH of the blood and so reduces the oxygen-carrying capacity through the Bohr effect on the haemoglobin (WOOD and LENFANT, 1976).

Simultaneous measurements of blood lactate and oxygen consumption suggest that in very active lizards, anaerobic glycolysis is responsible for between 50 and 90% of energy production. Exhaustion occurs rapidly, because of the depletion of creatine phosphate stores and the accumulation of lactic acid. A running lizard is capable of short bursts of speed, but it cannot sustain them. This limitation can be put to use in attempting to catch lizards in the field. For example, the small lizard *Psammodromus hispanicus* which lives on the sand dunes behind many of the beaches of the Mediterranean coast of France and Spain, has a home range centred on isolated thick tufts of bushy vegetation. When disturbed, the lizard runs very rapidly to the shelter provided by the nearest bush; it knows exactly where to go and so is very difficult to capture. But if it can be 'headed off' so that it must run across the bare sand, it very quickly loses momentum and, exhausted by a sprint of a few metres, can be picked up quite easily. Dependence upon anaerobic respiration for 'flight or fight' is clearly a disadvantage for reptiles, and some physiologists have speculated that a reduction in this dependence was the main selective advantage which favoured the evolution of endothermy. The family Varanidae is a modern group of lizards which perhaps represents an intermediate stage in the sequence. Varanid lizards are able to utilize oxygen during violent activity at a faster rate than others, partly because they have more complex lungs with a relatively large surface area and partly because they have high concentrations of myoglobin. In addition, the lactate which is produced does not cause the pH of the blood to fall, because this change is buffered. This difference is illustrated in Fig. 3-5 which shows the relation of blood pH to temperature in active sand goannas, *Varanus gouldii*, compared with the relationship in active spiny chuckwallas, *Sauromalus hispidus*, which belong to the family Iguanidae. Buffering in varanid lizards is not due to the bicarbonate-carbonic acid system found in mammals and birds

$$H^+ \text{ lactate} + Na^+ \ HCO_3' \rightleftharpoons Na \text{ lactate}' + CO_2 + H_2O,$$

because the concentration of carbonate does not change. It is now believed that the buffer is a protein.

Evolution of homeothermy can thus be seen as a process which might have occurred in two stages. The first was the development of behavioural thermoregulation as a means of raising and controlling

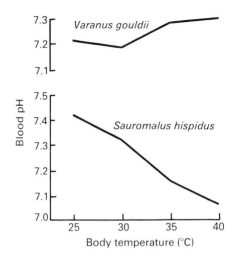

Fig. 3-5 Blood pH in relation to temperature in active sand goannas (*Varanus gouldii*) and spiny chuckwallas (*Sauromalus hispidus*). (Modified from BENNETT, A. F. (1973). *Comp. Biochem. Physiol.*, **46A**, 673–90.)

body temperature. Once this had become precise and reliable, many enzyme systems would become adapted to function with optimum efficiency at the PBT. A gradual increase in the contribution of endogenous metabolic heat, together with the development of insulation (fur, feathers and subdermal fat) to conserve it and endocrine and neurological mechanisms to control it (HARDY, 1976), could then follow.

Endothermic animals have achieved a considerable degree of independence from fluctuations in the physical environment, and this obviously gives them a competitive advantage. But it also involves a cost –that of maintaining the high metabolic rate. They must eat more and they must eat fairly continuously, if they are to survive. The problem is crucial for smaller endotherms, because they lose heat most rapidly. The voraciousness of shrews is well-known, and small birds also feed at prodigious rates; it has recently been calculated that a pied wagtail (*Motacilla alba*) must eat on average one small fly every four seconds throughout daylight hours to sustain its metabolism during the winter. Detailed studies on the bullfinch have shown that the birds lay down subcutaneous fat each day to act as fuel for the night. If a bullfinch (*Pyrrhula pyrrhula*) is prevented from feeding for more than a few hours on a cold winter morning, it utilizes all of the reserve and dies. Lizards do not have this kind of problem: they can be placed in the refrigerator for short periods and are always perfectly healthy when they are removed again! A hibernating lizard may survive for eight months without food and unlike a hibernating mammal it does not appear to need to modify its normal metabolism in order to do so.

This balance of benefit and cost may help to explain how lizards and snakes have succeeded in coexisting and even increasing for more than fifty million years of evolution alongside the mammals and birds. They may occupy the same habitat and may compete for the same sources of food, but they function in a different way.

4 Thermoregulation in Dinosaurs

Dinosaurs were the dominant vertebrates from the end of the Triassic until the end of the Cretaceous–a period of about 140 million years. For much of this time the climate was warm and stable. Many people have speculated that some dinosaurs might have been effectively homeothermic, if only because the rate of heat loss from the larger species, with their favourable surface: volume ratios, must have been small. The smaller species were almost certainly shuttling heliotherms or thigmotherms. It has been suggested that some of the large dinosaurs and other early reptiles were endothermic (see BAKKER, 1972). This is an attractive idea, because many species appear to have had an upright gait; they presumably moved fairly fast and it is difficult to see how a lizard-like physiology could supply the necessary energy at a sufficiently high rate. But if the animals were endothermic, they might have faced the problem of overheating during exercise. This has been overcome in mammals primarily by the development of sweat glands, and in birds by loss of heat from extensive extensions of the lungs called lung sacs. It may be that the spectacular 'sails' and other ornaments in such genera as *Stegosaurus* from the Upper Jurassic and Cretaceous, and *Dimetrodon* (Fig. 4-1) from the Permian, might have been giant heat-exchangers which functioned in a similar way to the skin of *Iguana*, as described in the last chapter. This supposes that the vascular supply to the 'sails' could be controlled –something we shall probably never know. *Dimetrodon* was not a dinosaur, but belonged to a group of reptiles called the Pelycosauria, which are usually considered to be very closely related to the ancestors of mammals.

There are several other arguments which support the hypothesis,

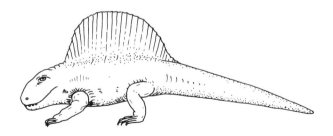

Fig. 4-1   Reconstruction of *Dimetrodon*, showing the dorsal 'sail'.

but none of them is conclusive. One is that the histology of the bones of dinosaur limbs is more like that of mammals and birds than that of lizards and other modern reptiles. Another is that the ratios of predatory carnivorous species to their herbivorous prey in any geological formation tend to be small. This would be expected if predatory dinosaurs were endothermic, since each individual would need far more prey than if it were ectothermic, for the reasons explained in Chapter 3. This 'palaeoecological' argument has been criticized on the grounds that the number of animals of different kinds which has become fossilized does not necessarily reflect either their relative abundance or their relative contributions to the energy flow in the ecosystem; the latter would also depend on difference in longevity and population turnover. Finally, if dinosaurs were primitive endotherms with rather poor insulation (and there is no evidence that they possessed fur or feathers, and a great deal that they did not), then they would have been more susceptible than ectotherms to the climatic upheavals which are believed to have occurred at the end of the Cretaceous. Endothermy might help to explain the dramatic extinction of the group at that time.

5 Thermoregulatory Adaptations in Hot Environments

5.1 Deserts

One of the characteristic features of desert environments in the tropics and subtropics is that temperatures fluctuate between wide extremes. Air temperatures of 40–45°C are common during the hottest part of the day and they may rise to more than 60°C. The desert surface, which usually has only the sparsest of vegetation cover, may at 60–70°C be so hot that it is painful to touch. But during the night, temperatures fall rapidly and by dawn the air may be distinctly chilly (i.e. below 10°C).

Deserts cover about one third of the land surface of the earth and a large number of animal species lives in them. Desert animals must be able to avoid overheating, have the ability to conserve water, and be able to withstand water loss if it should occur. Reptiles are well-

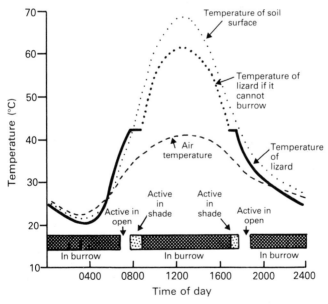

Fig. 5-1 Predicted activity and body temperature of a desert iguana (*Dipsosaurus dorsalis*) on July 15 at Palm Springs, California. (Modified from PORTER *et al.*, 1973.)

placed to meet these conditions and lizards in particular are amongst the most abundant of desert vertebrates. The basic features of the thermoregulatory behaviour of desert lizards are similar to those described in Chapter 2; but during the hotter parts of the day it is cooling, rather than heating, which becomes the paramount problem. The obvious way of cooling is to seek shade, beneath rocks or in burrows. Hence the daily activity pattern is bimodal, with peaks during the early morning and later afternoon.

An example is illustrated in Fig. 5-1, which shows the activity of a desert iguana, *Dipsosaurus dorsalis*, during mid-summer at Palm Springs in California. The lizard is active between 0715–0845 and 1730–1830 hours. The figure also shows environmental temperatures and body temperatures of the lizard; the latter are derived from the predictions of a very detailed mathematical model of the behaviour and thermal relations of *D. dorsalis*, which was constructed by a group of biologists and engineers at the University of Wisconsin (PORTER, MITCHELL, BECKMAN and DE WITT, 1973). Measurements in the field have shown that the iguanas maintain active body temperatures (PBTs) between 38 and 43°C. Using this data, the model can predict the activity of the lizards throughout the year. The prediction is shown in Fig. 5-2; it assumes that there are always cloudless blue skies and uninterrupted sunshine. The lizards must seek shade when

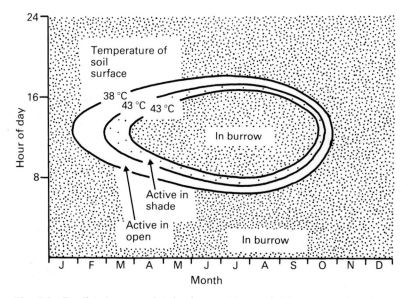

Fig. 5-2 Predicted seasonal behaviour patterns of *Dipsosaurus dorsalis* at Palm Springs, California. (Modified from PORTER *et al.*, 1973.)

the surface temperature rises above 43°C, but until it reaches this temperature in the shade they can still remain active.

Figure 5-2 consequently shows four categories of behaviour: inactive in the burrow at night (air temperature is too cool for activity); active in the open (the lizard can balance heat gains and heat losses to maintain the PBT); active in the shade (the PBT can still be maintained provided that heat gains are smaller than heat losses); inactive in the burrow during the day (air and surface temperatures are too high for activity). Note that the animal needs to spend at least a part of the day sheltering from excessive heat, for seven months of the year (April to October). The actual behaviour of the lizard fits the predictions of the model quite well, and if the model is modified to allow for additional variables such as vagaries in the weather, seasonal changes in the PBT, and the availability of bushes into which the animal can climb to avoid the hot desert surface, it becomes even more accurate. Figure 5-2 also shows that the time which is available for essential activities, such as hunting for food and capturing it, is quite small: for much of the year it is only about three hours per day. This is true for many species of desert lizards and so there has been a strong selection pressure for the evolution of morphological, physiological and behavioural adaptations which enable this time to be maximized.

One of the most important of such adaptations is a high activity temperature. It has already been noted that active *D. dorsalis* in California have body temperatures between 38 and 43°C. The desert dragon (*Amphibolurus inermis*) of Australia maintains equally high temperatures during hot weather; in the Simpson Desert the mean recorded body temperature was 41.5°C and in the region of Alice Springs 39.7°C (HEATWOLE, 1970). These temperatures are nearly lethal. In the laboratory, *A. inermis* will live for only eight hours at 44°C; they lose coordination almost instantly at 48.5°C and are killed by a brief exposure at 49.3°C. Other species within this genus maintain slightly lower temperatures; in the mallee dragon (*A. fordi*) from New South Wales, the recorded mean was 36.9°C, and in the bearded dragon (*A. barbatus*) it varied from 32 to 35°C in different parts of the geographical range. But the lethal temperatures of these species are lower too (46°C).

The margin of safety for lizards which maintain such remarkably high body temperatures is small. This disadvantage is offset by the fact that a high body temperature reduces dependence on heat sinks; the animals can remain active for longer periods before needing to cool. Other physiological adjustments include cutaneous vascular changes which reduce the rate at which heat is gained, and panting, which increases the rate of heat loss. Panting, however, is usually a last resort, because it also involves a considerable loss of water.

Table 3 Reflectivity of excized dorsal skin of three species of lizards from desert habitats compared with similar data for four species from forest or scrubland habitats. The table also shows the calculated rate of heating of each species in hot sunshine. (Adapted from HUTCHISON, V. H. and LARIMER, J. L. (1960). *Ecology*, **41**, 199–209. Copyright 1960 by the Ecological Society of America.)

	Average % reflectivity 400–1100 μm	Average heat gain from solar radiation $J cm^{-2} min^{-1}$
Desert species		
Dipsosaurus dorsalis	30.6	3.1
Phrynosoma platyrhinos	35.0	2.9
Sceloporus magister	15.4	3.8
Non-desert species		
Sceloporus undulatus	11.4	4.0
Anolis carolinensis	11.5	4.0
Podarcis (= *Lacerta*) *muralis*	7.6	4.1
Iguana iguana	6.2	4.2

Many desert lizards are able to change colour. Their skin is dark when the air is cool, and this increases the heating rate whilst the animals are basking. As they reach their activity temperature, the skin becomes paler; this is of value during the heat of the day because absorption of heat is reduced and so the time which elapses before the animals must seek shade is increased. It also helps to camouflage the lizards against the background glare of the desert soil. Measurements have shown that the reflectivity of the skin of desert lizards is greater than that of lizards from other habitats. This is illustrated in Table 3, which shows the mean reflectivity of the skin to wavelengths from 400–1100 μm. The table also shows heating rates of the animals in hot sunshine, calculated from the measurements of albedo (the reflectivity to all wavelengths); the desert species gain heat far less rapidly. The experiments were performed with a spectrophotometer using excized pieces of skin, with a block of magnesium carbonate as a standard, and so the figures only give an indication of the *relative* differences between the species. It is much more difficult to measure the albedo of a living lizard, although this has now been achieved. The differences in reflectivity recorded in Table 3 are not just due to differences in colour between the species; other properties of the dorsal skin surface must also differ, but this aspect has not yet been investigated in detail.

Observations on the behavioural adaptations of lizards have been

Fig. 5-3   Horned toad (*Phrynosoma platyrhinos*). (Photograph by courtesy of M. A. Linley.)

carried out in most of the major deserts of the world. HEATH (1965) at the University of California, in one of the earliest of such studies, worked on horned toads *Phrynosoma* spp. (Fig. 5-3). These are found in the hot, arid climates of the south-west of the U.S.A. and in the adjacent parts of Mexico. They burrow in loose, sandy soil during the night and also during the hotter parts of the day. Other thermoregulatory behaviour patterns include orientation (see Fig. 2-7) and colour change; and at very high temperatures, bulging eyes, panting, discharge of urine from the cloaca, and alterations in the body shape. The latter are effected by pulling the ribs backwards; this makes the animal deeper and slimmer, reducing the surface area which is exposed to direct sunlight. Heath measured these areas by photographing the shadow which was cast by the animal in the apparatus shown in Fig. 5-4 and measuring it with a planimeter. The figure shows a typical result, in this case for the species *Phrynosoma coronatum*. The inter-relationships of the entire repertoire of thermoregulatory behaviour in a horned toad are shown in Fig. 5-5.

Phrynosoma are squat, rather flattened lizards with relatively short limbs. Many of the more active desert lizards with longer limbs may raise their bodies off the ground in order to reduce heat conduction from the hot surface. The mallee dragon is an example of a lizard which does this. It has been studied in New South Wales by COGGER

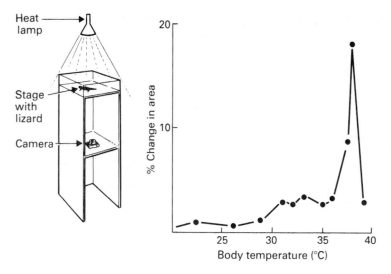

Fig. 5-4 Apparatus for measuring the shadow cast by a lizard, and hence the body area exposed to the sun: and a typical result, showing how the exposed body area changes with temperature in *Phrynosoma coronatum*. (Modified from HEATH (1965). With the permission of the University of California Press.)

(1974). Mallee dragons are found only in areas which have thick clumps of porcupine grass (*Triodia scariosa*) and the work is interesting because it illustrates how the behaviour of the lizards is influenced by the microclimate within the clumps: they shelter within these at night and bask near them in the morning and early evening, but once they have warmed up, they avoid them. As the soil surface becomes hot, cooling behaviour is seen more and more frequently. The head and body are raised by extending the front limbs so that the foreparts are supported on the tips of the claws. The hind parts of the body are supported on the heels, the digits are extended upwards at a sharp angle and the tail is raised well off the ground. If the surface becomes so hot that the body temperature rises above 39–40°C, the animals seek shade, either by burrowing or by returning to the bigger *Triodia* clumps (Fig. 5-6). The effectiveness of this behaviour may be appreciated by comparing temperatures at 1430 hours on a hot afternoon in January:

ambient air 44.7°C
substrate temperature 69.5°C
temperature within the porcupine grass clump 41.3°C

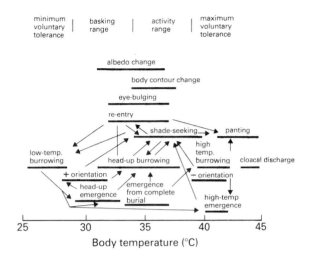

Fig. 5-5 Behaviour patterns which are concerned with thermoregulation in *Phrynosoma coronatum*, showing the range of temperatures at which each pattern occurs. (HEATH (1965). With the permission of the University of California Press.)

If a lizard is prevented from entering a clump or burrowing at this time, it dies within a few minutes. There is very little other shade.

A further problem which desert reptiles face is that of conserving water. The adaptations which serve to reduce water-loss are mostly physiological and the interested reader is referred to CLOUDSLEY-THOMSON (1971) and to a series of papers on the chuckwalla (*Sauromalus obesus*) in the Mojave Desert (references in NAGY and SHOEMAKER, 1975). There is one aspect, however, which deserves mention here. During a shower of rain, desert lizards may sometimes be seen in a basking posture and they appear to be soaking up water into the skin; if water is sprinkled onto them in the laboratory, they increase in weight. It was thought for many years that lizards could actually absorb water through the skin in this way. Some species may be able to do so – the evidence is rather inconclusive – but in the spiny devil, *Moloch horridus*, the mechanism is more subtle. The water does not pass through the skin, but along capillary spaces on the surface, and some of it reaches the corners of the mouth. The animals secrete mucus from labial glands; this absorbs the capillary water and is then licked off by the tongue and swallowed. This mechanism was confirmed experimentally by placing a dehydrated spiny devil in water

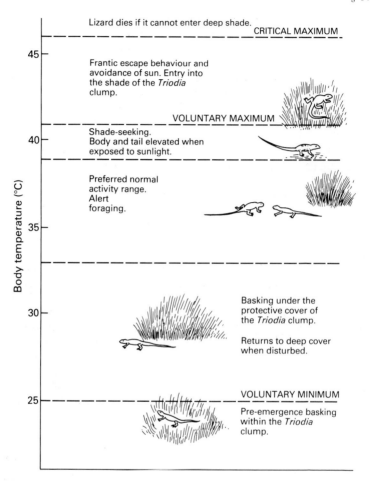

Fig. 5-6 Activity patterns at different body temperatures in the mallee dragon (*Amphibolurus fordi*). (Modified from COGGER, 1974.)

containing a colloidal dye, Evans blue; the coloration appeared in the stomach, even when the head was kept out of the water and the animal was prevented from drinking (BENTLEY and BLUMER, 1962).

5.2 Tropical forests

Tropical forests are amongst the most productive habitats, having an enormous diversity of ecological niches: animals may live on the forest floor, on the trunks of the trees, at many different levels in the branches, or high in the canopy, exposed to sunlight 50 m or more above the ground. More species of lizards are found in tropical forests than in any other kind of habitat, and include such interesting forms as the 'flying dragons' (*Draco* spp.) and the gliding gecko (*Ptychozoon homalocephalum*) from South East Asia. Little is known about most of these species, even though they may be very abundant. The densest lizard population which has ever been recorded is in a tropical forest, on the island of St Croix in the Virgin Islands. It is a single-species population of *Anolis acutus* and there may be as many as 5000 individuals per hectare in some areas. RUIBAL and PHILO-BOSIAN (1974) have shown, by 'mark-and-recapture' techniques, that a single tamarind tree may contain a resident population of 80 adult lizards.

One of the characteristic features of most tropical forests is that the climate is very stable. At Lamto, in the Ivory Coast, the mean monthly minimum temperatures fluctuate between 18 and 24°C and the maxima only between 26 and 31°C. The two commonest species of lizards in the forests of Lamto are skinks, *Mabuya blandingi* and *Panaspis kitsoni*. They have been studied by BARBAULT (1974), who showed that *M. blandingi* is a heliotherm, and so must seek patches of sunshine in order to bask, and its mean activity temperature is 33.4°C. *P. kitsoni*, on the other hand, does not bask and although the body temperature is usually close to that of the ambient air, the environment is sufficiently warm and stable for the lizard to be able to maintain a mean activity temperature of 27.1°C for considerable periods. Some species, such as *Anolis allogus* which lives near the forest floor of the dense jungles of Cuba, actually avoid sunshine, and in captivity these animals always remain in the darkest part of their cage.

6 Thermoregulatory Adaptations in Cool Environments

6.1 High altitudes

Perhaps the most severe climate in which lizards can be found is that of the high Peruvian Andes. One species, *Liolaemus multiformis*, extends above 4500 m (15000 ft). Lizards may also be found at great altitudes in the Caucasus Mountains; *Lacerta agilis* has been recorded at 4290 m (14 400 ft). This is a particularly interesting species because it also occurs at sea level, in the south of England and over much of Central Europe: the suburbs of Bournemouth are ecologically very different from the alpine pastures of Mount Elbrus!

Liolaemus has recently been studied in detail by monitoring its body temperature with a radiotelemetry device implanted into the body cavity. On a typical day during the summer, an adult lizard emerges from its crevice or burrow about two hours after sunrise. The air temperature at this time is near freezing and there may be snow on the ground. But by positioning itself on a mat of thick vegetation, which insulates it from the cold ground, and by basking for two hours, body temperature is raised to between 32 and 34°C and is maintained for a further two hours – the exact time depends on the cloud and snowstorms which tend to develop over the high peaks during the afternoons, which cause the animals to retire. PEARSON and BRADFORD (1976) made a careful analysis of the time which a lizard devoted to various activities (Table 4). More than 80% of the total time was spent inactive in the burrow and nearly 16%, or $3\frac{1}{2}$ hours per day, in thermoregulating. Only 0.3%, less than 5 minutes, was spent feeding, although a further 26 minutes which the authors called 'social and travel', could have included looking for food. Pearson and Bradford conclude that *Liolaemus multiformis* '... possess no obvious, excep-

Table 4 Time spent by an adult *Liolaemus multiformis* on various activities. (Adapted from PEARSON and BRADFORD, 1976.)

	Heliothermy	Thigmo-thermy	Social and travel	Feeding	Under-ground
Percentage of day (approx.)	12.3	3.5	1.8	0.3	82
Minutes (approx.)	177.1	50.4	25.9	4.3	1180.8

tional anatomical modifications to ease their existence in the extreme climate of the Andes...they are able to survive because their behavioural responses are well matched to the vicissitudes of the climate.'

6.2 High latitudes

Mean temperature, length of the summer, and intensity of solar radiation all decrease with increasing latitude. Conditions become less favourable for lizards; very few species occur in countries with cool, temperate climates (Table 5). Most of those which are found under such conditions nevertheless maintain high body temperatures; as in *Liolaemus multiformis*, thermoregulation plays an important part in their ecology and behaviour.

Table 5 The number of lizard species in some countries or states with temperate climates.

Location	Latitude	Number of lizard species
Iceland	63–67	0
Norway	58–72	3
England	50–56	3
Canada	49–70	4
West Germany	47–55	5
Tasmania	41–43	14
Kansas	37–40	14

The common lizard of Europe, *Lacerta vivipara* (Fig. 2-5), is found further from the Equator than any other species – its distribution extends north of the Arctic Circle. The PBT of this species is approximately 30°C (Table 1). This is three degrees lower than the temperatures of closely-related species from the south of Europe, and ten degrees lower than that of *Dipsosaurus dorsalis* from the deserts of California and Arizona. However, since air temperatures in northern Europe are cooler, it represents a considerable excess over ambient, and must be maintained by appropriate behaviour patterns. Individuals of *L. vivipara* will not feed efficiently if their body temperature falls below about 25°C. They must therefore spend much of their time in basking, especially when the sun is obscured by cloud, as it is so frequently in a temperate oceanic climate like that of England. Figure 6-1 shows how different kinds of cloud cover increase the heating-time of a basking *L. vivipara*; it can be seen that under many kinds of cloud, a lizard is not able to achieve its feeding temperature

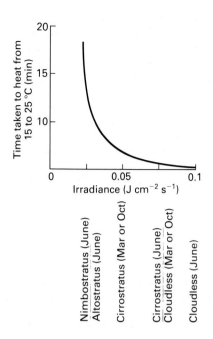

Fig. 6-1 The effects of various kinds of cloud cover on heating rates of *Lacerta vivipara*. (Modified with permission from AVERY (1976). Copyright by Academic Press Inc. (London) Ltd.)

at all. Weather conditions will consequently have an effect on feeding. Table 6 shows that the daily food intake of wild *L. vivipara* in England is lower than that of the related wall lizard *Podarcis muralis* in central Italy, where the climate is warmer and less cloudy. The mean daily intake in both species is reduced in cloudy conditions by nearly one half.

Table 6 Food intake by *Lacerta vivipara* in England, and *Podarcis muralis* in central Italy. (Calculated from data in AVERY, R. A. (1971). *J. Anim. Ecol.*, **40**, 351–65 and (1978) *J. Anim. Ecol.*, **47**, 143–58.)

Species	Weather	Food intake $(\mathrm{mg\,g^{-0.7}\,day^{-1}})$
L. vivipara	cloudy	38.2
	sunny	67.1
P. muralis	cloudy	59.4
	sunny	106.5

The maintenance of a high body temperature by ectothermic lizards in cool climates clearly involves a cost, since an individual must commit a considerable proportion of its total activity to thermoregulatory behaviour. The advantages of a high PBT, as discussed in Chapter 3, must be of greater importance than the loss of time for feeding, although the fact that body temperatures in *Liolaemus multiformis* and *Lacerta vivipara* are lower than those of many other diurnal lizard species shows that the evolution of an optimum strategy in these climates has involved a compromise.

Reduction of body temperature is not the only adaptation of lizards to life in cool climates. They also tend to become viviparous or ovoviviparous (HOGARTH, 1976), they may develop a placenta, they may produce their young or eggs only once every two years, and in some species the reproductive cycle may be modified to allow spermatozoa to be stored from one season to the next. The first of these allows the incubating eggs to be exposed to the heat of the sun (within the body of the basking female lizard) whilst at the same time be protected from predators; the remainder are adaptations which compensate for a low food intake by increasing reproductive efficiency, by allowing the synthesis of the large, yolky eggs to be spread over more than one season, or by allowing the young to be born early in the season so that there is time for them to accumulate adequate food reserves to support their metabolism during the long, cold winter.

6.3 Nocturnal lizards

There are many kinds of nocturnal lizards. They include the geckos (family Gekkonidae; see Fig. 6-2), which have a cosmopolitan distribution, and the night-lizards of North America (family Xantusiidae). Geckos are especially modified for activity after dark; the eye has a slit-like, vertical pupil, and the retina consists almost entirely of rods.

Nocturnal lizards are not able to thermoregulate actively during the night, and so their body temperature tends to follow that of the ambient air rather closely. Nevertheless, most of the species which have been examined have a well-defined PBT, which is usually within the range of 20–25°C. It is for this reason that many species are at their most active during the first three to four hours after sunset; as the air temperature falls, activity decreases. This is well-illustrated by the activity pattern of the gecko *Gehyra variegata* from New South Wales, in which careful studies have shown that the critical limit is an air temperature of 18°C. A typical record of the activity of this species is shown in Fig. 6-3; it was made with an aktograph, a piece of apparatus which can be constructed quite easily in the laboratory (see BUSTARD and GRANT, 1969; CARTHY, 1966). Investigations of the behaviour patterns of other species of geckos would make an

Fig. 6-2 Moorish gecko (*Tarentola mauritanica*). (Photograph by courtesy of M. A. Linley.)

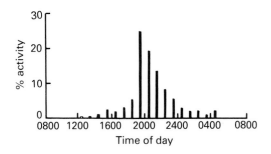

Fig. 6-3 Mean activity (expressed as hourly percentages of the total time) of twenty Australian geckos (*Gehyra variegata*) in an aktograph maintained out of doors in New South Wales. (BUSTARD, 1967.)

excellent experimental project. The behaviour of some species is more complex than that of *G. variegata*. For example, the common European gecko, *Tarentola mauritanica*, which is mainly nocturnal, may often be seen during the daytime in hot sunshine. The significance of this behaviour is not known; it might be associated with the breeding cycle, or with the availability of particular kinds of food. The factors which control behaviour cycles in nocturnal lizards may vary; in the tropics, it is often decreasing light intensity which appears to be the most important, whereas in cooler climates, temperature may also have a significant role. Some species are influenced by neither, and their rhythms may be endogenous.

7 Social Behaviour and Population Dynamics

7.1 Social behaviour

Many species of lizards have elaborate forms of social behaviour; these include courtship displays, and aggressive posturings which help an individual to defend a territory against intruders without always having to fight. Territories may have a number of functions. Often they represent an area in which an individual can feed without interference, and when female lizards defend a territory, this is probably the main reason. Territories may also be concerned with sexual selection; male lizards in particular usually use their territories to defend their mates.

Description and analysis of territory and its functions is at present a particularly active area of lizard research. There are many ways in which the problems can be studied experimentally. One of the simplest is to add individuals to, or remove them from, a wild population, and to observe what effects these manipulations have on territorial behaviour. A number of workers have supplemented the natural food of lizard populations with mealworms or flies, which have been bred in the laboratory for the purpose. In some species this appears to result in a reduction in the sizes of the territories which are held by individual animals, but in others it does not. An alternative

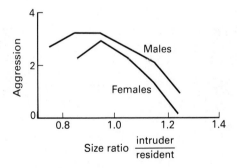

Fig. 7-1 Aggressive responses of male and female *Anolis aeneus* to individuals of the same sex in relation to the ratio of their difference in size (intruder/resident). Aggression was measured on an arbitrary scale in which different kinds of behaviour were given a numerical score. (STAMPS, J. A. (1977). *Ecology*, **58**, 349–58, Copyright 1977 by the Ecological Society of America.)

approach is to tether an individual in another's territory, and observe the response. The results of an experiment of this kind, carried out with *Anolis aeneus* in Granada, West Indies, are shown in Fig. 7-1. It can be seen that territory-holding lizards of both sexes are more aggressive to individuals which are smaller than themselves, and that males are more aggressive than females. Notice also that females are maximally aggressive towards females of approximately the same size, whereas males are almost equally aggressive to males which are the same size or smaller than themselves. This tends to support the hypothesis that females are competing primarily for food (since the greatest competition will be between individuals of the same size, which eat food within exactly the same range of sizes), whereas male aggression is also concerned with courtship and mating (since smaller males also represent a potential threat to the mate. Larger males may represent an even greater threat, but they are less likely to be challenged because of the probability that they will win the encounter.)

Lizards may have a large repertoire of behaviour patterns which act as signals to other individuals during courtship or defence of territory. A very common pattern, seen in a number of Agamidae in Africa, Asia and Australia, and in Iguanidae such as *Sceloporus* spp. (Fig. 7-2) in the Americas, is the 'bob', which involves rapid vertical move-

Fig. 7-2 Granite spiny lizard (*Sceloporus orcutti*). This animal has just completed a 'head bob' movement; the head and shoulder are raised well off the ground (compare *Lacerta vivipara* in Fig. 2-5). (Photograph by courtesy of M. A. Linley.)

ments of the head, often with 'press-ups' using the fore limbs. This behaviour has been studied by many workers, and there has been much speculation about its function (many Moslem people feel that in performing head bobs, agama lizards are mocking their ritual during daily prayers). BERRY (1974) made a very thorough study of the bobbing behaviour of chuckwallas (*Sauromalus obesus*) in California. She filmed thirteen individuals with a 16 mm camera, and analysed the sequences frame by frame. As a result of this painstaking work, she concluded that head bobs are used by male lizards under the following circumstances:

(a) *Assertion display* to advertize possession of a piece of ground or territory. The dewlap (a fold of skin beneath the throat) is not extended, and the presence of another lizard is not necessary to elicit the display.

(b) *Threat display*. This is only seen in the presence of another male lizard. The dewlap is usually extended, and the whole body is raised off the ground by straightening the fore and hind legs, as in Fig. 7-3c.

(c) *Courtship display*.

(d) *Challenge display*. This is seen only when two males of approximately equal size are in dispute. They align themselves laterally to one another, raise their bodies off the ground, extend their dewlaps, inflate their bodies by filling their lungs with air, so that they appear bloated (Fig. 7-3g), and then perform head bobs. Female lizards perform head bobs less frequently, although the behaviour is usually related to assertion or courtship.

Perhaps the most surprising finding of this study was that the way in which head bobs are performed varies slightly from lizard to lizard, but each individual tends always to perform in exactly the same way, especially during the first three or four seconds of the display. Berry was able to recognize the precise pattern of movement of some individuals as unique – she called it the signature. Examples of the analysis of displays by two male chuckwallas are shown in Fig. 7-4; the amplitude is the movement of the lizard's head in the vertical plane with respect to an arbitrary reference position. The first three traces show displays by an individual called male 80, and it can be seen that they are all very similar, and quite distinct from the displays of another individual, called by Berry 'Pen Tyrant', shown beneath them.

Not all species of lizards are territorial, nor do they all have aggressive or courtship displays. Many are solitary for the most part of their lives. In Europe, the species of diurnal lizards which live in the south, for example in Spain, Italy or Greece, show more complex

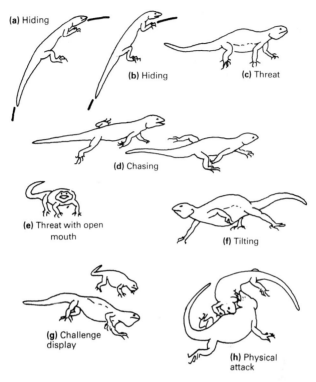

Fig. 7-3 Postures associated with aggression in the chuckwalla (*Sauromalus obesus*). (**a**) and (**b**) hiding, (**c**) threat, (**d**) chasing, (**e**) open-mouth threat, (**f**) 'tilting', (**g**) 'face-off' (two male lizards displaying laterally to one another, with heads lowered and backs arched), (**h**) attack. (BERRY (1974). With the permission of the University of California Press.)

patterns of social behaviour than those which inhabit northern countries like Britain and Scandinavia. This may be because the duration and intensity of solar radiation are lower in the north, and so the lizards which live there have to spend a longer time basking in order to achieve the PBT (Chapter 6). Complex social behaviour may therefore have adaptive advantage only for lizards in hot, stable climates (AVERY, 1976). There are several observations which support this hypothesis. Lizards which are found at very high altitudes or in fluctuating environments do not have highly-developed social behaviour. In the Mojave Desert, where the amount of rainfall varies enormously from year to year, chuckwallas abandon their social behaviour in very dry conditions when food is scarce (NAGY, 1973).

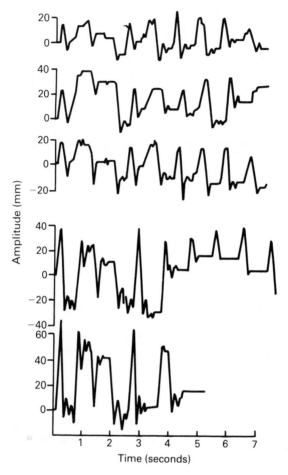

Fig. 7-4 Analysis of 'head-bob' movements in two male chuckwallas (*Sauromalus obesus*). (BERRY (1974). With the permission of the University of California Press.)

7.2 Population dynamics

The branch of zoology which has come to be called 'population dynamics' is concerned with the mechanisms which control the numbers of animals. It is a challenging field of study, because the factors involved are usually complex, and also because the animals themselves may be difficult to observe and capture. Lizards have proved easier to investigate in this respect than many other kinds of vertebrates. They can often be studied by direct observation, unlike many fishes, birds in a dense forest, or nocturnal mammals. Lizards can often be captured in large numbers with simple devices such as a noose mounted on a fishing rod, or pitfall traps manufactured from tin cans. They may be marked by clipping one or more claws in various combinations, and mark-and-recapture techniques (see SOUTHWOOD, 1978) have been used extensively in population studies.

The size of the population of a lizard species at any time is determined by the balance between birth rate (natality) and death rate (mortality). Lizards in the tropics tend to have higher birth rates than those in temperate climates, because they produce clutches of eggs at shorter intervals. There are many reasons for this. One of the most important is that more food is available in a tropical habitat. Another is that the individual lizard can spend more time at a high body temperature; food can be digested and utilized with maximum efficiency for longer periods. Lizards in the tropics consequently have more rapid growth rates. In addition, they do not need to store fat to provide metabolic fuel for winter hibernation, and so more energy is available for metabolism and growth.

But the pressures of competition and predation also tend to be higher in tropical environments, and so mortality rates are higher. It is characteristic of many smaller tropical lizard species that they breed early in life, they have high birth rates and high mortalities. In some, the mean expectation of life may be less than one year. *Anolis limifrons*, which is found in groves of banana and cacao trees in Costa Rica, is an example. The species was studied by FITCH (1973), who captured a large number of the lizards, and marked them by clipping toes, or with spots of quick-drying paint. He then captured further samples at intervals and showed that the proportion of marked individuals in the population fell exponentially, from 15% after two weeks to zero after six months.

Lizards in cooler climates, or in climates which fluctuate from season to season, are able to breed only once a year, and sometimes on even fewer occasions than this. They tend to survive for relatively long periods. Juvenile *Lacerta vivipara* which have been born in Britain in July or August, and which survive their first year of life, then have a further mean expectation of life of about five years, and some individuals undoubtedly reach more than ten years of age.

Appendix: Lizards in the Laboratory

A.1 Thermoregulation

Lizards of most species are comparatively easy to keep in the laboratory. Incorrect provision for their thermoregulatory needs is probably the commonest cause of failure; the principles discussed in Chapters 2 and 3 must be considered in designing accommodation for the animals. Many species from temperate and sub-tropical climates are heliotherms, and so need a source of radiant heat. A 250W chicken incubator lamp, suspended about 50 cm above the floor of the cage, and switched on for between four and eight hours per day, is suitable for a large cage; a 100W bulb is adequate for a smaller cage. The lizards must also have shade, so that they can lose heat when necessary; one way of providing this is to use sheets of thick cardboard folded as 'concertinas'. The periods of cool when the lamps are switched off are often just as important as the periods of heat: lizards from temperate climates which are allowed to remain *continuously* at their activity temperatures, often die. Non-basking lizards, which are mostly found in tropical areas, do not need a source of radiant heat, but for these the ambient air temperature must be kept high (25–30°C); these species are often susceptible to chilling if the temperature should fall.

A.2 Diet and water

It may be necessary to breed invertebrates in the laboratory to provide a constant supply of food. Crickets are particularly suitable, and they are easy to culture. Mealworms (larvae of the beetle *Tenebrio molitor*) are often used, but they should not be allowed to constitute a large part of the diet, because it is now known that their tissues have a very low ratio of calcium: phosphorus ions. If mealworms are fed for long periods, the excretion of excess phosphorus results in a hypocalcaemia, which leads to a progressive demineralization, and hence softening, of the bones (rickets). This problem is often exacerbated by a lack of vitamin D in the diet, and so a vitamin supplement may be helpful; this can be sprinkled on the food, or suspensions can be obtained to be added to the drinking water. Lizards which are exposed to natural sunlight are less likely to be deficient in vitamin D, because it can be synthesized in the skin under the influence of ultraviolet radiation. Normal glass filters out much of the ultraviolet; it can be replaced with a UV lamp, but care must be taken to ensure that the animals do not burn. The retina is particularly sensitive. Flourescent tubes can be bought which produce a light whose spectral composition is equivalent to that of sunlight, and so includes some UV radiation. These are excellent, but they do not provide adequate heat. They can often be purchased from aquarists' shops or horticultural suppliers.

Water must always be provided, but it must be given in a form in which the lizards would normally encounter it. Many species drink dew in the early morning, but never have access to standing water; for these, the drinking water must be sprayed on to surfaces in the cage. If this is not done, many species will die of dehydration, even though a dish of water may be available. Desert lizards may absorb water via the skin (Chapter 5).

A.3 Behaviour of captive lizards

However carefully the environment may be controlled, the behaviour of captive lizards is usually a much simplified travesty of behaviour which is seen in the field. It is a particularly instructive experiment to keep groups of individuals belonging to the same species in cages of different sizes. A smaller range of behaviour is usually seen in the smaller cages, especially if the species is normally territorial. Smaller cages may also result in behaviour patterns which are not usually seen in the wild: for example, if viviparous lizards (*Lacerta vivipara*) are crowded into a small cage, a dominance heirarchy which is equivalent to the 'peck order' seen in chickens, will develop. The largest animals feed first. In American 'chameleons' (*Anolis carolinensis*), which are arboreal, the social relationships which develop depend partly on the number of branches which are available as perches, and on their positions within the cage. Behavioural modifications of these sorts make excellent experimental projects; but if a 'peck order' is being investigated, care must be taken to ensure that the inferior individuals obtain enough food and do not starve.

The reproductive and other seasonal cycles of captive lizards are often disrupted. In temperate climates, a decision must be taken whether to allow the animals to hibernate during the winter, or to keep them active by maintaining the daily radiant heat and high air temperature. Lizards which would normally hibernate, and which are prevented from doing so, will not usually breed.

Further Reading

GANS, C. and TINKLE, D. W. (Eds) (1977). *Biology of the Reptilia*, volume 7, *Ecology and Behaviour A*. Academic Press, London, New York and San Francisco.

HEATWOLE, H. (1976). *Reptile Ecology*. University of Queensland Press, St. Lucia.

RICHARDS, S. A. (1973). *Temperature Regulation*. Wykeham, London and Winchester.

Illustrations of many of the species of lizards described in this book may be found in the following publications:

BURTON, M. and BURTON, R. (1975). *Encyclopaedia of Reptiles, Amphibians and Cold-blooded Animals*. Octopus Books, London.

PERKINS, L. (1974). *All-colour Book of Reptiles*. Octopus Books, London.

References

AVERY, R. A. (1976). Thermoregulation, metabolism and social behaviour in Lacertidae. In: *Morphology and Biology of Reptiles*, A. d'A. Bellairs and C. B. Cox (Eds). Linnean Society Symposium Series No. 3. Academic Press, London and New York.

AVERY, R. A. and MCARDLE, B. H. (1973). *Br. J. Herpetol.*, **5**, 363–8.

BAKKER, R. T. (1972). *Nature, Lond.*, **238**, 81–5.

BARBAULT, R. (1974). *Terre et Vie*, **28**, 272–95.

BARTHOLOMEW, G. A. and TUCKER, V. A. (1963). *Physiol. Zool.*, **36**, 199–218.

BENNETT, A. F. and DAWSON, W. R. (1976). Metabolism. In: *Biology of the Reptilia*, volume 5, *Physiology A*, C. Gans and W. R. Dawson (Eds). Academic Press, London, New York, and San Francisco.

BENTLEY, P. J. and BLUMER, W. F. C. (1962). *Nature, Lond.*, **194**, 699–700.

BERK, M. L. and HEATH, J. E. (1975). *J. Thermal Biol.*, **1**, 15–22.

BERRY, K. H. (1974). *Univ. Calif. Publ. Zool.*, **101**, 1–60.

BOGERT, C. M. (1949). *Evolution*, **3**, 195–211.

BUSTARD, H. R. (1967). *Copeia*, **1967**, 753–8.

BUSTARD, H. R. and GRANT, I. (1969). *Copeia*, **1969**, 843–7.

CAREY, F. G. and TEAL, J. M. (1969). *Comp. Biochem. Physiol.*, **28**, 205–13.

CARTHY, J. D. (1966). *The Study of Behaviour*. Studies in Biology no. 3. Edward Arnold, London.

CLOUDSLEY-THOMPSON, J. L. (1971). *The Temperature and Water Relations of Reptiles*. Merrow, Watford.

COGGER, H. G. (1974). *Austr. J. Zool.*, **22**, 319–39.

COWLES, R. B. and BOGERT, C. M. (1944). *Bull. Amer. Mus. Nat. Hist.*, **83**, 265–96.

FITCH, H. S. (1973). *Occ. Pap. Mus. Nat. Hist. Univ. Kansas*, **18**, 1–41.

HARDY, R. N. (1976). *Homeostasis*. Studies in Biology no. 63. Edward Arnold, London.

HEATH, J. E. (1962). *Science*, **138**, 891–2.

HEATH, J. E. (1965). *Univ. Calif. Publ. Zool.*, **64**, 97–136.

HEATH, J. E. (1966). *Physiol. Zool.*, **39**, 30–5.

HEATWOLE, H. (1970). *Ecol. Monogr.*, **40**, 425–57.

HOGARTH, P. J. (1976). *Viviparity*. Studies in Biology no. 75. Edward Arnold, London.

HUEY, R. B. and SLATKIN, M. (1976). *Q. Rev. Biol.*, **51**, 363–84.

NAGY, K. A. (1973). *Copeia*, **1973**, 93–102.

NAGY, K. A. and SHOEMAKER, V. H. (1975). *Physiol. Zool.*, **48**, 252–62.

PEARSON, O. P. and BRADFORD, D. F. (1976). *Copeia*, **1976**, 155–70.

PORTER, W. P., MITCHELL, J. W., BECKMAN, W. A. and DEWITT, C. B. (1973). *Oecologia, Berl.*, **13**, 1–54.

RAND, A. S. (1964). *Ecology*, **45**, 863–4.

RUIBAL, R. and PHILOBOSIAN, R. (1974). *Ecology*, **55**, 525–37.

SOUTHWOOD, T. R. E. (1978). *Ecological Methods.* 2nd edition. Methuen, London.

TURNER, F. B., MEDICA, P. A. and KOWALEWSKY, B. W. (1976). *Energy Utilization by a Desert Lizard*, Uta stansburiana. US-IBP Desert Biome Monograph no. 1, Utah State University Press, Logan.

WEESE, A. O. (1919). *Amer. Nat.*, **53**, 33–54.

WOOD, S. C. and LENFANT, C. J. M. (1976). Respiration: mechanics, control and gas exchange. In: *Biology of the Reptilia*, volume 5, *Physiology A*, C. Gans and W. R. Dawson (Eds). Academic Press, London, New York and San Francisco.